The New Leadership Code

The New Leadership Code

Insights through Case Stories

Biswaroop Mukherjee

ink | OCCAM

ISBN: 978-93-6547-376-6

First published in India 2025
This edition published 2025

BluOne Ink Pvt. Ltd
A-76, 2nd Floor, Sector 136, Noida
Uttar Pradesh 201301
www.bluone.ink
publisher@bluone.ink

Typeset in Adobe Garamond Pro by Manipal Technologies Limited
rinted and bound in India by Thomson Press (India) Ltd

Kali and Occam are imprints of BluOne Ink

ink | OCCAM

Contents

Introduction

Leadership is a journey, not a destination. It is a dynamic and evolving process that demands continuous learning, self-reflection, and adaptation. In a world where change is the only constant, developing effective leadership has never been more critical. Whether you are leading a global corporation, managing a small team, or simply striving to lead your own life with purpose and integrity, the principles of leadership remain universal—yet deeply personal.

This book invites you to explore the essence of leadership development. It is not merely about acquiring skills or adopting specific behaviours but about cultivating a mindset and way of being that inspire others to follow. The pages ahead will guide you through core leadership concepts, offering practical insights, real-world examples, and thought-provoking exercises to support your growth as a leader.

From my years of experience working with leaders across various sectors, one truth stands out: leadership is less about the power you wield and more about the influence you cultivate. True leadership is about empowering others, creating a shared vision, and fostering an environment where everyone can thrive. It requires leading with empathy, integrity, and a deep sense of responsibility.

This book is not just for those at the top of an organizational chart; it is for anyone seeking to make a positive impact within their sphere of influence. Leadership is not confined to a title—it is a way of living and engaging with the world.

As you embark on this journey, I encourage you to approach it with an open mind and a willingness to challenge your assumptions. As mentioned earlier, leadership is not a fixed destination but an ongoing process of growth. May this book serve as a valuable companion on your path to becoming the leader you aspire to be.

Let us begin this journey together, knowing that the world needs leaders who are not only capable but also compassionate, not only strategic but also empathetic, and not only successful but also deeply human.

Welcome to the journey of leadership development.

1

The Foundation of Leadership

The Leadership Development Model

The leadership development model discussed in this book is centred around the following image:

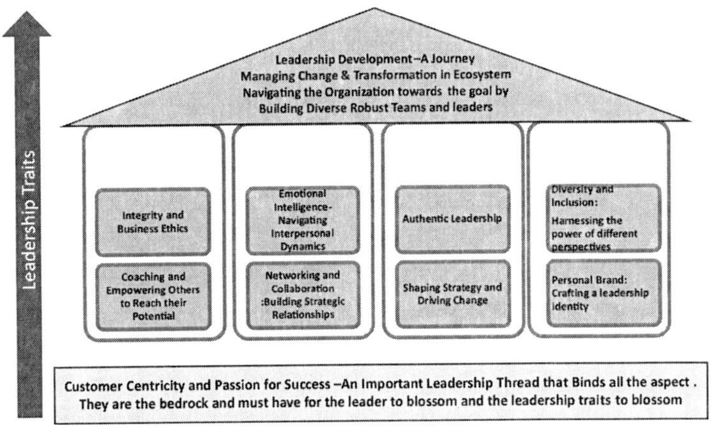

The image is a structured diagram in the shape of a house, representing the key elements of leadership development. The roof symbolizes the overarching goal of leadership—to manage change and transformation within the ecosystem; guide the organization towards its objectives; build diverse, resilient teams; and, most importantly, develop more leaders.

The concept of a leadership development house serves as a powerful visual representation of the multi-dimensional nature of leadership. Each block in the image represents a critical component that contributes to the overall strength and effectiveness of a leader. Let's explore these blocks in detail, examining their significance and how they interconnect to form a resilient leadership framework.

Integrity and Business Ethics: The Bedrock of Trust

At the heart of effective leadership lies integrity, the foundation upon which trust is built. Leaders who consistently uphold integrity make decisions that are honest, transparent, and aligned with their stated values. This consistency fosters trust among team members, stakeholders, and the wider community.

Business ethics, closely tied to integrity, ensures that decisions are not only beneficial in the short term but also sustainable and morally sound in the long run. Ethical leadership involves adhering to principles that promote fair treatment, compliance with laws, and respect for the rights of all stakeholders. Together, integrity and business ethics create a non-negotiable foundation that upholds all other leadership qualities.

Coaching: Empowering Others to Reach Their Full Potential

Coaching is a vital leadership skill that focusses on fostering the growth and development of others. Effective leaders act as coaches by providing guidance, feedback, and opportunities for professional advancement. They help team members recognize their strengths, address their weaknesses, and align their personal goals with those of the organization.

Coaching is not about giving orders but about asking the right questions, listening actively, and empowering others to take ownership of their roles. This approach cultivates a culture of continuous learning and improvement, which is essential for long-term success. By investing in their teams' development, leaders not only enhance individual performance but also strengthen the organization as a whole.

Emotional Intelligence: Navigating Interpersonal Dynamics

Emotional intelligence is the ability to understand and manage one's own emotions and those of others. Leaders with high emotional intelligence excel at recognizing emotional cues, managing stress, and resolving conflicts. They foster an environment where people feel understood, valued, and motivated.

Emotional intelligence is particularly crucial in leadership, as it shapes how leaders handle difficult conversations, inspire and motivate their teams, and cultivate a positive organizational culture. Leaders with strong emotional intelligence are better equipped to navigate the complexities of human relationships, which are at the core of any organization. By fostering trust, collaboration, and a sense of belonging, they create a strong foundation for team success.

Diversity and Inclusion: Harnessing the Power of Different Perspectives

In today's globalized and interconnected world, diversity and inclusion are not optional—they are essential for any organization that aims to thrive. Leaders who embrace diversity recognize that a range of perspectives fosters innovation and leads to better decision-making.

Diversity in leadership involves actively seeking and valuing different viewpoints, backgrounds, and experiences. Inclusion ensures that all voices are heard and that everyone feels they have a place at the table. This not only drives creativity and innovation but also enhances employee engagement and satisfaction. Leaders who prioritize diversity and inclusion are better equipped to guide organizations that reflect and serve an increasingly diverse world.

Networking and Collaboration: Building Strategic Relationships

Networking is a vital aspect of effective leadership, enabling leaders to build and maintain relationships that support and advance their goals. Through networking, leaders gain access to new ideas, resources, and opportunities that drive problem-solving, innovation, and organizational growth.

Effective networking goes beyond simply collecting business cards—it involves cultivating genuine relationships based on mutual respect and shared interests. Skilled networkers know how to leverage their connections to benefit their teams and organizations, whether by attracting top talent, securing strategic partnerships, or expanding into new markets.

Personal Branding: Crafting a Leadership Identity

Personal branding defines how a leader presents themselves to the world. It involves articulating and communicating one's unique value proposition—encompassing strengths, values, and leadership style. A well-crafted personal brand enhances a leader's credibility and influence, making it easier to inspire and guide others.

In today's digital age, where leaders are often visible to a global audience, personal branding is more important than ever. By cultivating a clear and consistent brand, leaders can build trust and rapport with their teams, stakeholders, and the wider public. This, in turn, creates new opportunities and strengthens their ability to drive change and achieve their vision.

Shaping Strategy and Driving Change

Effective leaders shape strategy and drive change by creating a compelling vision for the future and aligning organizational goals with market opportunities. Those who excel in this area are visionary thinkers who anticipate trends, adapt to challenges, and develop strategic plans that propel their organizations forward.

These leaders are adept at managing change, communicating effectively, and inspiring teams to embrace new directions. They balance long-term objectives with immediate needs, foster innovation, and ensure their teams are empowered and equipped to drive transformation—all while remaining agile in a dynamic environment.

Authentic Leadership

Authentic leadership is about being genuine, transparent, and true to one's values while guiding others. Leaders who embody authenticity are self-aware; they recognize their strengths, weaknesses, and emotions, and use this awareness to build trust and meaningful relationships with their teams.

They lead with integrity, staying true to their values and beliefs even in challenging situations. Authentic leaders are also empathetic, actively listening to others' perspectives, fostering open communication, and creating an environment where people feel safe to express themselves. By being transparent and trustworthy, they inspire loyalty, encourage collaboration, and cultivate a positive, inclusive workplace culture.

Customer Centricity

Customer centricity as a leadership trait is the ability to prioritize customers' needs, expectations, and experiences in every decision and strategy. Customer-centric leaders demonstrate empathy by deeply understanding their customers' pain points and aspirations, using feedback to enhance their experiences. They align organizational goals with delivering exceptional customer value, ensuring that every team contributes to this mission.

These leaders are innovative problem-solvers, anticipating customer needs and adapting to changing demands while holding themselves accountable for outcomes such as satisfaction and loyalty. They also empower their teams to act in the customer's best interest, fostering a culture of trust and advocacy. By consistently placing customers at the heart of their leadership, they drive sustainable growth and create a lasting competitive advantage.

Passion for Success

Passion for success is a crucial leadership trait that drives individuals to pursue their goals with determination and enthusiasm. It inspires leaders to overcome obstacles, innovate, and maintain a clear vision for the future. This inner drive not only fuels their own growth but also motivates their teams, fostering a culture of perseverance and excellence.

Leaders with a passion for success are deeply committed to their mission, and their energy is contagious, instilling resilience and a shared sense of purpose within the organization. This unwavering dedication often leads to transformative results, making passion a cornerstone of effective leadership.

Leadership Development: A Lifelong Journey

The roof of the leadership development house labelled 'Leadership Development' symbolizes the overarching need for continuous growth and learning. Leadership development is not a one-time event but an ongoing process that requires leaders to consistently seek new knowledge, skills, and experiences.

Effective leadership development involves self-reflection, seeking feedback, and being open to change. It also requires staying informed about industry trends, technological advancements, and global issues that may impact an organization. By committing to lifelong learning, leaders remain adaptable, innovative, and prepared to navigate the challenges and opportunities of an ever-evolving world.

Conclusion

The leadership development house serves as a powerful framework, illustrating the complexity and interconnectivity of the skills and qualities essential for effective leadership. By focusing on key components—integrity, coaching, emotional intelligence, diversity and inclusion, networking, personal branding, and leadership development—leaders can build a strong, resilient foundation that supports their growth and success.

This holistic approach ensures that leaders are not only equipped to meet the demands of their current roles but are also prepared to evolve and thrive in the future. Just as a house requires careful planning, construction, and maintenance to stand the test of time, leadership, too, demands continuous development, attention to detail, and a commitment to excellence. By embracing the principles embodied in the leadership development house, leaders can build a lasting legacy that inspires others to follow in their footsteps.

In the first part of this book, we will explore five of the ten topics in depth, drawing insights from case stories that illustrate each facet of leadership. These are case stories, not case studies, designed to bring leadership concepts to life through real-world narratives. Some attributes are interwoven within these stories, reflecting the interconnected nature of leadership.

The objective of this book is to offer readers glimpses into real-life situations that leaders encounter and the challenges they overcome on their journey. Through these stories, readers can reflect on their own leadership development and gain insights into the qualities that shape effective leaders.

2

Case Story 1
Integrity and Business Ethics

Balancing Ethics and Organizational Loyalty

It was raining heavily, and Naina had been staring at the downpour through the glass panes of her office in a tony suburb of Mumbai for quite some time. She wasn't merely watching the rain—she was lost in thought, grappling with a dilemma that had been weighing on her mind for a while. That day, however, it was no longer just a dilemma; it had become a source of deep distress.

Her thoughts drifted to the day she first walked into this office as a finance manager nearly ten years ago. She recalled how, with each passing year, she had grown in stature and how much she owed to this organization that had provided her with incredible opportunities to fulfil her aspirations and ambitions. She had been fortunate to work alongside great colleagues who had helped her learn, adapt, and grow within the company. Among them, the most influential had been her mentor and current boss, Mr Khanna.

It was Mr Khanna who had hired her when he was the head of the department. Over the years, he had risen to become the CEO, and Naina herself had climbed the ranks to become the CFO. Never, not even in her wildest dreams, had she imagined becoming the CFO within a decade of joining. As she gazed at the drizzling rain, a wave of gratitude washed over her—gratitude for the organization, for Mr Khanna, and for colleagues like Seema and Anup, whose unwavering support had shaped her journey.

The company she had joined and the company it had become were vastly different. It had grown multifold, and after the immense success of its new products, it had established itself as a formidable brand in both Indian and global markets.

As she continued staring at the rain, she felt the warmth of tears welling up in her eyes, blurring her vision and making the downpour seem even hazier. She was struggling to quieten the turmoil within her. She felt utterly lost, with no one to confide in. The immense gratitude she felt toward the organization made her reluctant to take any step that might jeopardize its fortunes—no matter how much she wrestled with the ethical dilemma gnawing at her conscience.

The dilemma for Naina had begun three months ago when Arpita joined as a new management trainee in her office. She was a young, eager learner, always enthusiastic about trying new things and brimming with curiosity. Naina often saw a reflection of her younger self in Arpita—energetic, curious, and full of life. The resemblance in their personalities made Naina feel a deep sense of affection and care for her.

Over time, they became friendly, often sharing their experiences of life and work despite belonging to different generations and having a significant age gap. They would typically catch up over lunch, exchanging food and stories.

One afternoon, a few months after Arpita joined, she arrived for lunch in an unusually sombre mood. Noticing her silence and low energy, Naina asked what was wrong. At first, Arpita remained quiet, but after some gentle probing, she confided in Naina. She said that Mr Khanna, the CEO, had been acting overly familiar with her, and earlier that day, under the pretext of appreciating her, he had touched her inappropriately—his hand lingering on her back. She had always held Mr Khanna in high regard and appreciated his support on her project, but for the past few days, she had noticed him looking at her in a way that made her uncomfortable. Today's incident had left her feeling uneasy and disheartened.

Naina was taken aback by what she heard. She had worked closely with Mr Khanna for a long time and found it hard to believe Arpita's interpretation of the incident. She told Arpita that Mr Khanna might have genuinely been trying to encourage her and that she could be reading too much into it. But Arpita was certain about his intent, even if it had been disguised under the pretext of appreciation.

After some discussion, they agreed to observe Mr Khanna's behaviour closely and update each other if anything similar happened again. While Naina felt Arpita might have been overreacting, she was glad they had talked about it, as she could counsel her. On the other hand, though Arpita remained unconvinced, she trusted Naina enough to consider that she might have misread the situation. Talking to Naina helped her feel a little bit better, and she decided to carry on with her day, though a lingering doubt remained in her mind.

Time went by, and the Annual Awards Night became the highlight of the season. Everyone at work eagerly awaited this day—not just for the recognition and entertainment but also for the sense of camaraderie it fostered. The evening included dinner, cocktails, and an open-air party by the sea, accompanied by lively music.

Both Arpita and Naina arrived at the event together. After the awards ceremony, Naina felt quite tired and decided to leave early after dinner. Arpita, full of youthful energy, stayed behind, dancing and celebrating late into the night. As Naina bid farewell to everyone and headed home, Arpita continued to enjoy the festivities.

The next morning, Naina arrived at work feeling a bit fatigued from the late night. As she was going through her emails, Arpita walked into her cabin and suddenly broke down in tears. Concerned, Naina asked her what was wrong. After sobbing for a while, Arpita finally opened up. She recounted how, after the party, she had been heavily intoxicated and barely able to walk. Seeing her in that state, Mr Khanna had offered to drop her home in his car. During the ride, she said, he had touched her inappropriately and, for a while, kissed her all over. She had been too drunk to resist, and the memory of the ordeal had been haunting her since she woke up that morning. She was deeply disturbed and wanted to file a complaint against Mr Khanna. She also no longer wished to work in the organization.

Naina found herself in an incredibly delicate situation. On one hand, she believed Arpita—she knew her to be genuine, and it was clear she had gone through something deeply unsettling. On the other hand, she also understood the gravity of the situation. Such an accusation would not only damage Mr Khanna's reputation but could also put the entire organization's future at risk.

While these thoughts raced through her mind, she focussed on calming Arpita down. She assured her that she would take the matter seriously and acknowledged that what Mr Khanna had allegedly done was wrong. She urged Arpita to trust her and, for the moment, not speak about it to anyone else. Naina was careful about this—she understood the serious ramifications of any loose talk.

As soon as Arpita left, Naina acted swiftly. She called Mr Khanna's secretary and requested an urgent meeting. Within five minutes, she was in his cabin. Mr Khanna, who had been reading a report, greeted her in his usual jovial manner. Noticing her troubled expression, he immediately asked her what the problem was. Naina told him that it was serious, which only made him more curious.

She then narrated everything Arpita had told her—both the incident from the previous night and the concerns Arpita had raised earlier. She emphasized that this was a serious ethical misconduct with potentially huge ramifications for him and the organization.

After listening to her, Mr Khanna simply smiled and dismissed the allegation, calling them false. He insisted that nothing of the sort had happened. He advised Naina to explain things to Arpita and, if she was still unwilling to let it go, encourage her to leave the organization. Investigating or reporting such baseless claims, he said, would only create unnecessary trouble for everyone. He then turned to Naina and reminded her of their long association. He asked whether she had ever witnessed such behaviour from him. He argued that while he had only tried to help Arpita, she was now framing him with false allegations. His advice was clear: handle the situation delicately and find a way to remove Arpita from the organization. However, if an investigation was necessary, he was prepared to face it.

Naina left his cabin with a heavy heart, caught in a deep dilemma. She didn't know whom to believe. She wanted to trust both of them, yet their accounts stood in stark contradiction. More than anything, she wished she wasn't in this situation at all.

As the day progressed, Naina's thoughts became clearer. She now had a better sense of the actions she needed to take. She called Arpita in and asked her to recount the events of the previous night in greater detail. Naina also wanted to know if Arpita had any proof to support her claims.

Arpita, already shaken by the incident, broke down again. She was taken aback by Naina's investigative approach—she had expected support, not questioning. But Naina was determined to pursue the truth and gain absolute clarity. As she probed further, it became clear that Arpita had no concrete evidence—only her personal experience of the ordeal. By the end of the day, Naina advised Arpita to treat the incident as an unfortunate experience and move on. She explained that without evidence, pursuing the matter could be detrimental not only to the organization but also to Arpita's future within it.

Arpita had great respect for Naina, which is why she listened to her advice. However, she left the room feeling hopeless and deeply sorry for finding herself in such a situation.

After that day, Arpita didn't come to work for a few days. When she finally returned two days later, it was to hand in her resignation. She told Naina that it was out of respect for their relationship that she had decided not to file a formal complaint and was following her advice. However, she made it clear that what had happened was not a figment of her imagination—it was a fact that Mr Khanna had molested her in the dark while she was in an inebriated state. Arpita also expressed her disappointment that, as a woman, Naina had not pursued the matter or supported her in taking action. At the same time, she acknowledged Naina's candour and pragmatism in handling the situation. Despite this, Arpita was firm in her decision—she no longer wished to work in the organization. She had lost respect for Mr Khanna and no longer felt safe in the workplace.

As Arpita walked out of the office, Naina felt a pang of guilt. Somewhere deep down, she began to believe Arpita's story—after all, why would she resign from her job if she hadn't truly experienced the ordeal? Staring out the window at the rain, Naina felt tears welling up in her eyes. She couldn't shake the feeling that she had let Arpita down, even though she had done everything with what she believed to be the organization's best interests at heart.

Points for Reflection

- What would you have done differently if you were in Naina's position?
- Did Naina's actions truly mitigate risk for the organization, and were they in its best interest?
- What would have been the ideal advice for Arpita when she first raised concerns about Mr Khanna?
- What measures should organizations take to prevent such situations, and how can they ensure a consistent and fair approach in handling them?
- If you were Arpita, how would you have navigated the situation to hold Mr Khanna accountable for his actions?

Author's Perspective on the Case Story

What would you have done differently if you were in Naina's position?

If I were in Naina's position, I would have prioritized both ethical responsibility and the well-being of employees and the organization. Ethical leadership requires making difficult decisions that uphold the integrity of the workplace, even when they are uncomfortable or may seem damaging in the short term. Dismissing or downplaying such concerns can foster a toxic work environment and erode trust within the organization.

Upon hearing Arpita's account, I would have taken her allegations seriously from the outset. I would have encouraged her to formally report the incident to HR or the ethics committee, ensuring that the matter was investigated thoroughly and impartially. Leadership should set the tone for ethical behaviour, demonstrating that no one is above accountability, regardless of their position. Addressing the issue transparently would reinforce a commitment to maintaining a safe and respectful workplace while also protecting the organization from potential long-term risks associated with ignoring such serious allegations.

Did Naina's actions truly mitigate risk for the organization, and were they in its best interest?

While Naina's actions may have temporarily avoided a scandal, they did not genuinely mitigate the organization's long-term risks. Ethical leadership is not just about preventing immediate crises but about fostering a culture of transparency, trust, and accountability. By failing to address the issue properly, Naina inadvertently exposed the organization to greater risks, including a loss of trust among employees, potential legal repercussions, and reputational damage if the situation were to become public in the future.

An organization's long-term stability depends on its leaders' willingness to confront uncomfortable truths and take corrective action, even when it involves senior executives. By failing to uphold ethical standards, Naina risked undermining the very values that had contributed to the organization's success.

What would have been the ideal advice for Arpita when she first raised concerns about Mr Khanna?

The ideal response from Naina would have been to take Arpita's concerns seriously and guide her through the proper channels for addressing such issues. Naina should have emphasized the importance of adhering to the organization's ethical guidelines and encouraged Arpita to:

- **Document the incident:** Advise Arpita to write down everything she remembers about the incident, including details such as time, location, and any potential witnesses.
- **Report to HR or the ethics committee:** Encourage Arpita to file a formal complaint through the appropriate channels within the organization, ensuring that her concerns are heard and addressed confidentially.
- **Seek support:** Offer her reassurance and guidance throughout the process, affirming that the organization is committed to maintaining a safe and respectful workplace for all employees.

By taking this approach, Naina would have demonstrated ethical leadership and reinforced the principles that all employees, regardless of their position, are held accountable for their actions.

What measures should organizations take to prevent such situations, and how can they ensure a consistent and fair approach in handling them?

To effectively prevent and address such situations, organizations must foster a culture of ethics, transparency, and accountability. Key measures include:

- **Clear ethical standards:** Establishing a comprehensive code of conduct that defines acceptable behaviour and the consequences of ethical violations, ensuring that all employees understand and adhere to these principles.

- **Leadership by example:** Encouraging leaders to uphold a model ethical behaviour, demonstrating that integrity is non-negotiable at all levels of organization.
- **Robust reporting mechanisms:** Implementing accessible and confidential channels for reporting misconduct, including anonymous options, to empower employees to come forward without fear of retaliation.
- **Consistent enforcement:** Ensuring that all complaints are investigated thoroughly and impartially, with appropriate consequences for those found guilty of misconduct, regardless of their position.
- **Regular training:** Conducting regular ethics training for employees, particularly leaders, to reinforce the importance of ethical behaviour and educate them on proper reporting procedures.

By implementing these measures, organizations can create a safe and inclusive workplace where ethical standards are upheld consistently.

If you were Arpita, how would you have navigated the situation to hold Mr Khanna accountable for his actions?

If I were Arpita, I would have taken a structured approach to ensure both my personal safety and ethical responsibility. My steps would include:

- **Documenting the incident:** Carefully recording every detail of the incident, including dates, times, locations, and interactions with Mr Khanna, to create a clear and factual account.
- **Seeking legal counsel beyond Naina:** Consulting a legal professional or an external advisor to understand

my rights, legal protections, and the best course of action rather than relying solely on internal guidance.
- **Filing a formal complaint:** Reporting the incident to HR or the organization's ethics committee, providing all available documentation to support my claim and ensure a proper investigation.

By taking these steps, I would work towards holding Mr Khanna accountable while also upholding the ethical integrity of the organization and ensuring a safer workplace for others.

The Role of Ethics in Leadership

Ethical leadership plays a pivotal role in shaping an organization's culture and long-term success. Leaders set the tone for workplace behaviour, influencing how decisions are made, how employees act, and how the organization is perceived both internally and externally. Ethical leadership goes beyond merely adhering to laws and regulations; it involves fostering a culture of honesty, transparency, and respect.

Leaders who prioritize ethics are more likely to build trust with employees, stakeholders, and customers. They create an environment where employees feel safe to voice concerns, knowing their issues will be addressed fairly and without bias. When leaders model ethical behaviour, they inspire others to do the same, fostering a more cohesive and motivated workforce.

In the case of Naina and Mr Khanna, ethical leadership would have required Naina to prioritize the well-being and safety of her employees over any potential repercussions. By failing to do so, she risked undermining the organization's ethical foundation, which could have long-term consequences for both employees and the company as a whole.

Organizations that prioritize ethics in leadership not only safeguard themselves against scandals and legal issues but also cultivate a positive work environment where employees are more likely to be engaged, productive, and loyal.

As a leader, driving ethical conduct within an organization requires focusing on several key aspects. By prioritizing these principles, you can foster a culture of trust, integrity, and accountability throughout your organization:

Personal integrity

- **Lead by example:** A leader's behaviour sets the standard for the entire organization; therefore, consistently demonstrate ethical conduct in actions and decisions, reinforcing that integrity is non-negotiable.
- **Accountability:** Take responsibility for actions, acknowledge mistakes when they occur, and ensure transparency in decision-making.

Clear ethical standards

- **Establish a code of conduct:** Develop and communicate a clear, comprehensive code of ethics that defines expected behaviours and reinforces the organization's values.
- **Consistency in enforcement:** Apply ethical standards uniformly across all levels of the organization,

ensuring they are upheld regardless of an individual's position or influence.

Communication

- **Transparency:** Foster a culture of open communication where employees feel safe to raise ethical concerns without fear of retaliation.
- **Regular dialogue:** Integrate discussions about ethics into regular meetings, training sessions, and internal communications to ensure ethical considerations remain a priority.

Training and education

- **Regular training:** Provide ongoing ethics training for all employees, including leaders, to reinforce the importance of ethical behaviour and ensure everyone stays informed about ethical policies and procedures.
- **Scenario-based learning:** Use real-world examples and hypothetical scenarios to help employees apply ethical principles in their daily work.

Support systems

- **Ethics committees or officers:** Appoint dedicated ethics officers or committees to oversee the organization's ethical conduct, address complaints, and ensure policies remain current.
- **Whistleblower protections:** Establish and promote confidential reporting mechanisms for unethical behaviour while safeguarding whistleblowers from retaliation.

Fair and consistent consequences

- **Zero tolerance for unethical behaviour:** Clearly communicate that unethical conduct will not be tolerated and ensure consistent, fair consequences for violations of ethical standards.
- **Corrective action:** Address ethical breaches swiftly and appropriately, implementing corrective measures to prevent recurrence.

Stakeholder consideration

- **Respect for all stakeholders:** Make decisions that account for the impact on all stakeholders, including employees, customers, shareholders, and the broader community. Ethical leadership requires balancing these interests fairly.
- **Corporate social responsibility (CSR):** Support CSR initiatives that align with the organization's ethical values, fostering positive contributions to society and the environment.

Cultural alignment

- **Embedding ethics into organizational culture:** Ensure ethical values are deeply integrated into the organization's culture by incorporating ethics into performance reviews, reward systems, and overall business strategy.
- **Encouraging ethical behaviour:** Recognize and reward employees who demonstrate strong ethical conduct, reinforcing the message that ethics are a core organizational value.

Continuous improvement

- **Regular audits and assessments:** Conduct periodic audits and assessments of ethical practices and policies to identify areas for improvement.
- **Feedback loops:** Establish mechanisms for continuous feedback from employees and other stakeholders on ethical practices, using this input to make necessary adjustments.

Long-term vision

- **Sustainable decision-making:** Ensure decisions adhere to ethical standards in the short term while also considering their long-term impact on the organization and society.
- **Ethical innovation:** Encourage innovation within ethical boundaries, ensuring that new products, services, or business models contribute positively to the organization and its stakeholders.

By focussing on these aspects, leaders can not only drive ethical conduct within their organization but also foster a culture of trust, respect, and integrity that supports long-term success.

3

Case Story 2 Authentic Leadership

Two Styles of Leadership

Mayank and Ajit were both business heads in the same organization, of similar age, tenure, and career progression—though they had climbed the corporate ladder through different paths. Despite these similarities, their leadership styles were markedly different.

Being a business head was a demanding role, and both were adapting to the challenges it brought. They were performing well and were considered strong contenders for the CEO position. Mayank had risen through the sales ranks to become a business head, whereas Ajit had followed a techno-commercial path to reach the same leadership level. Mayank was charismatic, exuberant, and energetic—what you see is what you get. In contrast, Ajit was reserved, poised, and polished, a leader who thought more than he spoke. An introvert by nature, he preferred to keep to himself and maintained a composed demeanour.

Riya, a marketing leader who had worked under both Mayank and Ajit at different points in her career, succinctly captured their differences. She described Mayank as the most authentic leader she had worked with, while Ajit stood out as the most emotionally intelligent. She valued her experiences with both, appreciating their distinct leadership styles in different ways.

Did this mean Ajit was not authentic? Was he someone who was not real? Riya clarified that Ajit possessed a high level of emotional intelligence, which enabled him to manage his emotions carefully and remain contextual and restrained in how he addressed problems, situations, or people. In contrast, Mayank was direct, upfront, and always spoke his mind. His emotions were clearly visible, whether in moments of success or challenge.

Riya further illustrated the difference between the two with examples. She noted that Mayank's feedback to his subordinates was always direct. With him, there were no surprises—she always knew what to expect, whether good or bad. Even when he gave her tough developmental feedback, she genuinely felt it came from a place of encouragement. She believed he wanted her to improve, rise, and shine, which made her appreciate his directness. In fact, she always looked forward to his guidance, as she knew he genuinely cared for her growth and development.

That was Mayank's strength and charisma—he knew how to have his way, but he also knew how to win hearts in his own style. While he never compromised on doing the job the right way or hesitated to call out underperformance, he was equally invested in developing his team members. His genuine care for their growth set him apart. Riya mentioned that even today, despite working in different organizations within the same group of companies, she still sought feedback from Mayank, valuing his insights and mentorship.

With Ajit, the situation was different in this regard. Riya recalled that she often had to deal with surprises, primarily because Ajit rarely voiced unpleasant feedback directly. As a result, she sometimes missed the key points needed for course correction or adjustments in her approach to solving a problem or addressing a situation.

It was difficult for her to gauge what was on Ajit's mind—whether before an appraisal discussion, an important product launch, or a media briefing. While Ajit was a thorough gentleman and always ensured she had the necessary information and guidance to deliver on a project, there were times when things didn't go well. In those instances, she felt that if Ajit had clearly expressed his concerns earlier, the outcome could have been much better.

A similar issue arose during appraisal discussions. Ajit would often bring up an incident from months ago and provide feedback on how she could have handled it differently. However, since he had not voiced any concerns at the time, she missed the opportunity to clarify or make corrections then and there. This left her unsure of whether the delayed feedback would negatively impact her rating.

Another aspect of Ajit's leadership that frustrated her was his tendency to acquiesce to the company's CEO, often aligning with the CEO's perspective without much resistance—even when she knew Ajit initially held a divergent view. This led to complete rework for Riya and her team, requiring them to redraw their entire strategy.

In contrast, this was an aspect of Mayank's leadership that she admired. Unlike Ajit, Mayank would openly debate with the CEO, reasoning through his views and often managing to convince the CEO of his approach. While there were instances where he ultimately adjusted his strategy based on the CEO's feedback, it was always after a thorough discussion in which both perspectives were explored and understood. Even when she had to revise her approach after these discussions, Riya felt a sense of satisfaction—Mayank ensured that all ideas were considered, evaluated, and reasoned before making a final decision.

With such different leadership styles, both Mayank and Ajit were successful in similar roles. This often made Riya wonder what kind of leader she should be when she eventually reached the CEO position in her career. Should she adopt Mayank's authentic, charismatic, and energetic leadership style, or should she emulate Ajit's emotionally intelligent, restrained, and poised approach?

As she reflected on their personalities and her experiences with both, she struggled to reach a conclusion—after all, both had achieved success in their own ways. But then, she had a realization. Even after so many years, she still looked up to Mayank, stayed connected with him for feedback and advice, and knew many others who swore by his leadership.

What stood out most about Mayank was his ability to create leaders. Over the course of his career, he had mentored and developed numerous individuals who had gone on to excel within or outside the organization. While Ajit, too, had many admirers and those who respected him as a leader, their relationship with him remained professional and somewhat restrained.

Through this internal debate, Riya gained a profound insight—while the business world may measure a leader's success in financial terms and the ROI they deliver to stakeholders, a leader's true legacy lies in their authenticity, the impact they leave on their followers, and the guidance, experience, and growth they provide to those they lead.

Points for Reflection

- What does authentic leadership truly entail?
- Are emotional intelligence and authentic leadership opposites?
- Is leadership about building a legacy beyond numbers and profits?
- Managers at higher roles are not always regarded as leaders. Does this mean leadership is an act rather than a role?
- Leaders inspire, guide, and enable. How can they do this more effectively? Through coaching, mentoring, or guiding? What other approaches might be effective?

Author's Perspective on the Case Story

What does authentic leadership truly entail?

Authentic leadership is about being genuine, transparent, and true to one's values and beliefs. It involves leading with integrity, openly sharing thoughts and emotions, and aligning actions and intentions. A leader like Mayank builds trust through consistency in words and actions, fostering an environment of openness and direct communication. Authentic leadership cultivates trust and respect, as followers feel they are engaging with someone sincere rather than a leader hiding behind a façade.

Key aspects of authentic leadership are as follows:

- **Transparency:** Open and honest communication.
- **Self-awareness:** Understanding and reflecting on one's values, strengths, and weaknesses.
- **Relational transparency:** Building trust through genuine and honest interactions.
- **Consistency:** Aligning actions with core values and leading by example.

Are emotional intelligence and authentic leadership opposites?

Emotional intelligence and authentic leadership are not opposites; rather, they complement each other. As mentioned earlier, emotional intelligence involves the ability to understand and manage one's own emotions and those of others—an essential skill for building relationships, making decisions, and leading effectively.

While Ajit demonstrated high emotional intelligence, particularly in managing his emotions and interactions, this did not necessarily make him less authentic. In fact, emotional intelligence can enhance authentic leadership by enabling leaders to navigate complex interpersonal dynamics with empathy and awareness. However, a lack of transparency or the withholding of emotions, as Ajit sometimes did, may create a perception of inauthenticity.

Key aspects of emotional intelligence in leadership are as follows:

- **Self-regulation:** Controlling or redirecting disruptive emotions and impulses.
- **Empathy:** Understanding the emotions and perspectives of others.
- **Social skills:** Managing relationships to guide and influence others effectively.
- **Self-awareness:** Recognizing and understanding one's own emotions and their impact.

Is leadership about building a legacy beyond numbers and profits?

Leadership is not just about financial success or delivering results—it is about the legacy a leader leaves behind. This legacy is shaped by the impact on their team, the culture they create, and the leaders they develop along the way.

Mayank's legacy, as described by Riya, lay in the leaders he had nurtured and developed, many of whom continued to seek his guidance even after moving on. This highlights the enduring influence of authentic leadership. In contrast, while Ajit was successful and respected, he might not have built the same depth of lasting relationships, which affected the legacy he left behind.

Key components of a leadership legacy are as follows:

- **Impact on people:** How a leader develops and influences others.
- **Cultural influence:** The environment and values a leader instils in the organization.
- **Sustainable success:** Creating systems and structures that endure beyond the leader's tenure.
- **Long-term relationships:** The lasting connections and influence a leader maintains over time.

Managers in higher roles are not always regarded as leaders. Does this mean leadership is an act rather than a role?

Leadership is not defined by a position or title—it is demonstrated through actions, influence, and the ability to inspire and guide others. While both Mayank and Ajit held senior managerial roles, their approaches to leadership differed, shaping how they were perceived by their teams.

A manager may have authority, but a leader earns respect and loyalty through their actions, decision-making, and interpersonal approach. Mayank's authenticity made him more relatable and inspiring, strengthening his leadership in the eyes of his followers. Ajit, though successful, might be seen more as a manager due to his reserved and less transparent style.

Key distinctions between managers and leaders are as follows:

- **Authority vs influence:** Managers rely on authority; leaders inspire and influence.
- **Task-oriented vs people-oriented:** Managers focus on tasks and processes; leaders prioritize people and development.
- **Short-term vs long-term visions:** Managers often focus on immediate goals; leaders think beyond, shaping long-term impact and legacy.

Leaders inspire, guide, and enable. How can they do this more effectively? Through coaching, mentoring, or guiding? What other approaches might be effective?

Leaders can inspire, guide, and enable their teams through various approaches, including coaching, mentoring, and providing clear guidance. Both Mayank and Ajit had strengths in this area, though their methods differed. Mayank's direct and transparent feedback helped his team members understand their performance and expectations clearly, which could be highly empowering. Ajit's emotionally intelligent approach allowed him to address individual needs effectively, though it might sometimes lack the clarity that directness provides.

Strategies for effective leadership are as follows:

- **Coaching and mentoring:** Regularly engage with team members to develop their skills and support their growth.
- **Providing clear feedback:** Offer direct, honest, and constructive feedback while maintaining a supportive approach.
- **Empowering others:** Delegate responsibilities and trust team members to take ownership of their work.
- **Continuous learning:** Foster a culture of continuous improvement and learning, both for the leader and the team.

Conclusion

Riya's reflections on Mayank's and Ajit's leadership styles provide valuable insights into the diverse approaches leaders can take. While both have been successful, their contrasting styles highlight the significance of authenticity and emotional intelligence in leadership. Authenticity fosters deep, lasting relationships and a strong legacy, while emotional intelligence ensures these relationships are managed with empathy and awareness.

Ultimately, effective leadership requires a balance between authenticity and emotional intelligence. Leaders must adapt their style to the needs of their team while remaining true to their core values. Those who can integrate both approaches are best positioned to inspire, guide, and enable their teams, leaving a lasting positive impact on their organizations and the people they lead.

4

Case Story 3 Emotional Intelligence

Struggle with Workplace Dynamics

Roger was the HR leader of a large conglomerate, responsible for managing diverse stakeholders in the sales and marketing function. His client group was varied—comprising both seasoned and new employees, right-brained creatives and left-brained analysts, polished marketeers and straightforward sales leaders. He had them all in his pack.

Roger had joined the organization a few years ago, and since then, he had been on a constant treadmill. His challenges ranged from supporting the company's growth aspirations to integrating HR systems with business processes to enhance employee experience. He also had to develop policies to attract millennials while addressing legal and compliance issues—some of which were legacy problems that required extra time and effort to resolve.

Despite these demands, Roger brought extensive functional experience to the role and was able to drive key outcomes effectively. While the relentless pace of work took a toll on him, he found it engaging and satisfying. He thrived on creating new frameworks, driving high performance, and, most importantly, achieving targets and milestones, which gave him a strong sense of accomplishment.

However, one aspect of his role that Roger wished had been different was his team. He managed a large group of mid- and junior-level employees who had operated without a leader for nearly six months before he joined. In that time, they had developed their own ways of working and manging stakeholders. When Roger arrived with a clear mandate for business imperatives the team was unfamiliar with, his push for change was met with resistance. The more he tried to drive transformation, the more they pushed back, requiring significant time and effort to align them with his vision.

Fortunately for Roger, there was one exception in the team—a mid-level manager named John. John had been hired around the same time as Roger, specifically to drive change management. Unlike the others, John was open to transformation, and the two quickly developed a strong working relationship. In John, Roger found a valuable sounding board to navigate the challenges of organizational change, even as the rest of the team remained resistant.

The demanding business scenario, a resistant team unwilling to drive change and transformation, and multiple stakeholders with differing perspectives—all of this was adding to Roger's stress. While he enjoyed the challenge, his drive to achieve results ruffled more feathers than necessary, both among stakeholders and within his team. The resulting friction eventually reached the CEO and CHRO.

Both leaders were aware of the context in which Roger was operating, as well as the breadth of experience and value he brought to the organization. Recognizing the need of intervention, they decided to have separate one-on-one discussions with him, taking a counselling approach to ensure he remained motivated while also encouraging him to reflect on and constructively address the feedback.

Although these sessions were intended as a soft course correction, Roger took them very seriously—and was devasted afterward. He felt that despite his best efforts to drive the organizational agenda, he was being unfairly singled out. When he had joined, there had been no proper handover, his team had not been supportive, and numerous unresolved issues had required significant effort on his part. Yet, instead of acknowledging these challenges, the organization appeared unsympathetic to his side of the story. He believed that even though he took steps to address the resistance within his team or to align disengaged leaders with the company's objectives, he was the one being asked to change.

The feeling of being lost in the battle lingered in Roger's mind. He felt agitated inside and had been unable to focus on his work for the past few days. Noticing the change in his demeanour, John approached him and asked about his altered behaviour and the troubled expression he had been wearing.

As their conversation progressed, Roger began confiding in John about his frustrations. He expressed his belief that some team members and stakeholders, driven by their own selfish motives, were trying to tarnish his reputation with senior leadership. He felt this was because he had confronted them directly while pushing his transformation agendas.

John listened patiently and then reasoned with Roger, explaining that such resistance is common in large-scale transformations. He advised Roger to take the feedback from leadership in stride, adapt where necessary, and navigate the challenges ahead without adding to the noise that had already caused disruption.

Talking to John and sharing his thoughts made Roger feel lighter. He took some of John's advice to heart, felt a bit better, and went home that day in a much better frame of mind than when he had arrived at work.

As time passed and the transformations began taking shape, the noise within the organization grew louder. Rumours spread about Roger becoming increasingly adamant and hot-headed. There had been instances where he walked out of meetings in frustration or lost his temper, directly confronting stakeholders who resisted change—even to the point of yelling at them.

Adding fuel to the fire was Erica, a seasoned mid-level HR manager who had been with the organization for some time. Before Roger's arrival, she had enjoyed significant attention from senior leadership. However, with Roger now leading the team and making bold moves, she not only resisted the changes but also actively spoke out against Roger—both within the team and to senior leaders she had access to.

Sensing an opportunity to undermine Roger, Erica began openly criticizing him. She claimed he was not inclusive, was overly demanding, and frequently lost his temper with the team, creating an environment of stress and humiliation. Her vocal opposition further intensified the negative perception forming around Roger.

Everything that was happening made Roger increasingly uncomfortable. The stress was mounting—on one side, he had work deliverables and the challenge of rallying the organization through a transformative journey; on the other, he faced resistance from stakeholders, team politics, and bosses who did not seem to understand his perspective. The narrative about him was growing more negative, painting him as adamant, inflexible, lacking empathy for stakeholders, and emotionally immature.

One evening, feeling overwhelmed, Roger decided to take John out for coffee. He wanted to share his side of the story and seek John's opinion on how he could improve the situation. His sleepless nights had taken a toll, and he needed to confide in someone who could understand his workplace struggles.

After a few cups of coffee, Roger finally opened up. He shared the challenges he was facing, the way the narrative around him was being shaped, and how people like Erica, who were against him, were seizing the opportunity to escalate the situation even further.

John was an experienced professional who had navigated both life and organizational challenges himself. Though he hadn't risen as quickly as Roger, they were the same age, and he could relate to Roger's frustrations, anger, and sadness. In short, he understood the range of emotions consuming Roger.

As Roger finished sharing his story, John paused briefly before asking a question that stayed with Roger for a long time. He asked Roger to describe his feelings in more detail. That simple prompt led Roger to open up further—sharing how he had joined the organization with great aspirations, how he had been delivering results, and how he had initially thrived on the challenges. The more he spoke, the deeper he delved into the reasons behind his frustration and sense of dejection.

As Roger expressed his emotions, John continued to ask uncomfortable questions—challenging his assumptions about stakeholders who opposed him and team members who seemed to be working against him. Through this conversation, Roger had a realization—he had been fixated on achieving outcomes strictly on his terms. He recognized that he had not been flexible enough to navigate uncertainty alongside his stakeholders and team. He saw that he had been unwilling to bend or consider others' perspectives with empathy.

More importantly, he realized his self-awareness was lacking. What John had helped him see about himself was something he should have reflected on earlier. This newfound awareness led Roger to start regulating his behaviour—in meetings, in difficult situations, and in his daily interactions. His conscious effort to approach situations with poise and grace became noticeable to those around him.

The more Roger regulated his behaviour, the more his stakeholders began to perceive him as empathetic. They noticed that he was making an effort to understand their perspectives, and in turn, they became more open to his viewpoints. The same transformation took place within his team. The positive shift in workplace energy—both with stakeholders and his team—reinvigorated Roger. He was regaining his confidence and slowly realizing the true power of emotional intelligence.

Emotional intelligence rests on four pillars: self-awareness, self-regulation, empathy, and social skills. It is a crucial leadership trait with a significant impact on shaping a successful leader. Roger had to learn this lesson the hard way, but thanks to his reflections with John, he was able to change course and get back on track. However, emotional intelligence does not have to be learnt through struggle alone—it can be consciously developed by building oneself around these four pillars.

Points for Reflection

- What is emotional intelligence?
- If Roger had been more emotionally intelligent, how might he have approached the transformation differently?
- Was John emotionally intelligent? If he had a high emotional quotient, why was he not growing as quickly as people like Roger, who had lower emotional quotient?
- What are the best ways to develop and manage emotional intelligence?
- Why is emotional intelligence particularly important in today's corporate world?

Author's Perspective on the Case Story

What is emotional intelligence?

Emotional intelligence is the ability to recognize, understand, and manage our own emotions and the emotions of others. It consists of four key components:

- **Self-awareness:** Recognizing one's emotions and understanding their impact.
- **Self-regulation:** Managing emotions and adapting to changing circumstances.
- **Empathy:** Understanding and sharing the feelings of others.
- **Social skills:** Building and managing relationships to influence and inspire others.

These components enable individuals to navigate social complexities, lead effectively, and achieve both personal and professional success.

If Roger had been more emotionally intelligent, how might he have approached the transformation differently?

Had Roger possessed a higher level of emotional intelligence, he might have approached the transformation in the following ways:

- **Self-awareness:** He would have recognized his stress and frustration early on and taken steps to manage these emotions before they negatively impacted his interactions.
- **Self-regulation:** He would have demonstrated greater patience and flexibility, allowing his team and stakeholders more time to adapt rather than pushing for immediate results.
- **Empathy:** By understanding the perspectives and concerns of his team and stakeholders, he could have fostered a more collaborative and less confrontational approach.
- **Social skills:** He would have focussed on building stronger relationships and trust, which could have

reduced resistance and increased support for the transformation.

Was John emotionally intelligent? If he had a high emotional quotient, why was he not growing as quickly as people like Roger, who had lower emotional quotient?

John demonstrated emotional intelligence by empathizing with Roger, asking insightful questions, and guiding him towards self-reflection. However, career growth in a corporate environment depends on multiple factors beyond emotional intelligence. Possible reasons why John was not advancing as quickly as Roger include:

- **Risk aversion:** John may have been more cautious in his career, avoiding conflicts or challenges that could have accelerated his growth.
- **Lack of ambition or networking:** He might not have actively pursued promotions or visibility within the organization as aggressively as Roger did.
- **Organizational politics:** In some workplaces, factors such as political acumen or alignment with influential leaders can have a great impact on career progression than emotional intelligence alone.

What are the best ways to develop and manage emotional intelligence?

To master and manage emotional intelligence, individuals can:

- **Practice self-reflection:** Regularly assess one's emotions and their impact on decisions and relationships.

- **Seek feedback:** Actively solicit input from peers, mentors, and subordinates to gain different perspectives on one's behaviour.
- **Develop empathy:** Engage in active listening, consider situations from others' viewpoints, and be mindful of non-verbal cues.
- **Manage stress:** Adopt coping mechanisms such as mindfulness, exercise, or hobbies to handle stress and prevent it from affecting professional interactions.
- **Build relationships:** Invest time in fostering strong, trust-based connections with colleagues and stakeholders.

Why is emotional intelligence particularly important in today's corporate world?

In today's corporate environment, where collaboration, innovation, and leadership are essential, emotional intelligence is increasingly recognized as a key driver of success. Leaders with high emotional intelligence are better equipped to manage teams, navigate complex interpersonal dynamics, and drive change in a way that inspires and motivates others. In a rapidly evolving workplace, the ability to adapt emotionally, maintain positive relationships, and handle challenges with resilience can distinguish successful leaders from those who struggle.

Conclusion

Roger's experience highlights the critical role of emotional intelligence in leadership. By reflecting on his behaviour and developing his emotional quotient, he improved his relationships, reduced conflict, and regained his effectiveness as a leader. This case story underscores the value of emotional intelligence in navigating corporate challenges and achieving long-term success.

5

Case Story 4 Continuous Self-development

The Rise and the Stagnation

John was one of the brightest leaders in the company. He received ample exposure, recognition, and rapid promotions to various leadership roles well ahead of his time. Everyone in the organization looked up to him as an inspiration because of his career trajectory, body of work, the recognition he received, the perks he enjoyed, and the aura he emanated.

Several leaders served as his sponsors, enabling his growth because they believed in him and witnessed his rise from strength to strength. The young boy they hired straight from school turned out to be a terrific asset to the organization in the long run. While those leaders eventually moved on, John continued to thrive for some time—thanks to the quality of his work and, more importantly, the reputation he had built.

In recent times, however, John faced significant challenges and felt increasingly frustrated because the new chief of the organization did not perceive him as highly as he had been rated over the years. Moreover, John was unwilling to change his style or approach problems differently from the way he believed was right. His team also found him rigid and autocratic. Some who had known him for years observed a shift—from a high-energy, optimistic, and talented youngster to a more rigid and authoritarian leader. Many of his newer team members were hesitant to be candid with him and felt it was safer to align with his views rather than challenge them. In short, team engagement declined.

As a result, John's performance deteriorated day by day. Once a star who consistently excelled, he struggled to deliver, leading to mounting pressure from the CEO. Additionally, team engagement scores reflected a lack of alignment and motivation, further explaining the drop in performance.

John was in despair and had been feeling low for some time. He had never faced such a situation in his professional career. This was the first time in his decade-and-a-half-long career that he experienced a low phase, and his workplace had suddenly become a source of stress. Despite his untiring efforts to bring about change, he struggled to achieve his goals and found neither success nor luck.

This situation likely resonates with many of us. We have seen many Johns—whether as their managers, subordinates, or peers. How could we help John? How could he address these challenges and get back on track? There was much that John brought to the organization, and if he regained his footing, he could continue to be a valuable asset.

In a coaching conversation, John spoke endlessly about his successes—the glory, the belief, the pride, and the wins. This reflection helped him realize that his continued success had reinforced strong belief systems, which had now become his biggest challenge.

For several sessions, every conversation and anecdote reeked of pride and an attitude of 'been there, done that'—to the extent that it became almost obnoxious. However, the more he spoke, and the more his behaviour was examined, the clearer it became to him—he had indeed developed an overwhelming sense of self-pride and a know-it-all attitude.

He began to recognize that his ability to adapt, learn, and navigate ambiguity had significantly declined. His resistance to approaching old problems with fresh perspectives limited his effectiveness. Gradually, he started to understand his team's feedback about his autocratic style and unwillingness to change. He also realized why his manager was frustrated—he was attempting to solve new problems using outdated methods that had worked in the past but were no longer effective. He realized that success had a flip side—he was now facing the consequences of sustained success, something he had always aspired to and never anticipated.

What happened to John—how he coped with his low phase, how coaching helped him get back on track, and the struggles he endured to transform into the leader he needed to become—perhaps that is a story for another day. However, what is important now is to reflect on a few key insights for individuals navigating their careers and for organizations managing talent:

- Success breeds confidence, but it also reinforces strong beliefs that can create resistance to change. The stronger these beliefs become, the more they foster a know-it-all attitude.

- A leader's sponsorship and belief in someone can create credibility and success, but it often overlooks development areas. When a leader fully trusts a person's talent, they may fail to challenge them. Organizations and individuals must test talent with different leaders and contexts to enable continuous growth and adaptability. Development gaps should be identified early, allowing time for improvement rather than being exposed in high-intensity roles where immediate success is expected.
- Having a sounding board—a group of team members, sponsors, mentors, and friends—who provide unfiltered feedback on achievements and areas of development is invaluable for continuous growth.
- Beware of 'yes men' or 'yes women' in your team—they are one of the biggest drawbacks for a leader. They reinforce false beliefs and create blind spots. Encourage candid discussions, embrace constructive criticism, and listen to those who challenge your decisions—it may lead to better solutions.
- Most importantly, take your title a little less seriously. The more seriously you wear your badge, the further you distance yourself from the 'man in the arena', losing touch with the realities on the ground where the real action happens.
- The ability to embrace failure and emerge stronger is a crucial leadership skills. Pushing young leaders into different terrains early in their careers helps them develop resilience and adaptability.

- Lastly, when in self-doubt or struggling to navigate a challenge, seek the guidance of a certified coach. Sometimes, a coach's perspective and structured reflection can be the catalyst for the turnaround you need.

Points for Reflection

- If you were John and had just started your career, how would you have crafted it differently?
- What do you think were the top three reasons John ended up in a difficult spot, and how should he now overcome them?
- If you identify a 'John' in your team, how would you approach the discussion with him differently after reading this case?
- What structural mechanism should organizations put in place to prevent their top talent from facing challenges like the one John encountered? What tools can organizations use to better manage high-potential employees, especially fast-trackers?
- Do you think John should have received coaching much earlier? How should organizations design executive coaching programmes for high-potential talent?

Author's Perspective on the Case Story

If you were John and had just started your career, how would you have crafted it differently?

If I were John at the start of my career, I would focus on the following strategies to avoid the pitfalls he encountered:

- **Continuous learning and adaptability:** From the outset, I would cultivate a mindset of continuous learning, ensuring that I remain open to new ideas, feedback, and industry changes. This would involve regularly updating my skills and approaches rather than relying solely on past successes.

- **Building diverse relationships:** I would actively build relationships with a variety of leaders and mentors within the organization to gain different perspectives. This would help me avoid becoming overly dependent on the views and validation of a single sponsor.
- **Self-reflection and feedback loops:** Seeking regular feedback from peers, subordinates, and mentors would be a priority. I would develop a habit of self-reflection, consistently evaluating my decisions and leadership style to prevent a rigid mindset from taking hold.

What do you think were the top three reasons John ended up in a difficult spot, and how should he now overcome them?

The top three reasons are:

- **Over-reliance on past success:** John's inability to adapt and modify his methods to suit new challenges and contexts led to his struggles. He depended too much on past successes without recognizing that different situations require different approaches.
- **Lack of diverse feedback:** John's growth was primarily shaped by a few sponsors, limiting his perspective on his abilities. This lack of diverse feedback reinforced his rigid leadership style and prevented him from recognizing his own shortcomings.
- **Inflexibility and autocratic behaviour:** Over time, John became less receptive to feedback and more

autocratic, which alienated his team and resulted in lower engagement and performance.

To overcome these challenges, John should:

- **Embrace coaching:** John should continue with coaching to enhance self-awareness and emotional intelligence. Through coaching, he can identify and dismantle his rigid belief systems.
- **Engage with the team:** John needs to rebuild trust and foster open communication with his team. Encouraging candid discussions and actively listening to feedback will help re-engage his team and improve overall performance.
- **Adopt a growth mindset:** John should develop a growth mindset, viewing challenges and failures as opportunities to learn and evolve. This shift will enable him to adapt more effectively to new situations.

If you identify a John in your team, how would you approach the discussion with him differently after reading this case?

If I were to identify a 'John' in my team, I would approach the discussion with the following strategies:

- **Start with empathy:** I would begin the conversation with empathy, acknowledging that the individual may be going through a challenging period. Recognizing their past successes and contributions would help build rapport and create a supportive environment for discussions.
- **Focus on self-reflection:** I would encourage them to reflect on their current challenges and consider whether their approach needs to change. Asking

open-ended questions that prompt self-assessment can be a powerful way to initiate this process.

- **Introduce the concept of adaptability:** I would highlight the importance of adaptability in leadership by sharing examples of how successful leaders have evolved over time. Framing the conversation around growth rather than criticism would help them see change as an opportunity rather than a setback.

What structural mechanisms should organizations put in place to prevent their top talent from facing challenges like the one John encountered? What tools can organizations use to better manage high-potential employees, especially fast-trackers?

To ensure that top talent continues to grow without facing setbacks like John's, organizations should implement the following measures:

- **Regular development assessments:** Organizations should implement regular assessments that evaluate not only performance but also adaptability, emotional intelligence, and openness to feedback. These assessments can help identify potential issues before they become critical.
- **Mentorship and diverse sponsorship:** Instead of relying on a single mentor or sponsor, organizations should encourage high-potential employees to engage with multiple leaders. A diverse mentorship network provides a broader perspective and fosters well-rounded development.
- **Structured coaching programmes:** Implementing structured coaching programmes for high-potential

employees can help them navigate leadership challenges. These programmes should be proactive, starting early in the employee's leadership journey rather than waiting until problems emerge.

- **Feedback mechanisms:** Establishing safe, anonymous feedback channels where team members can share concerns about leadership styles without fear of repercussions is essential. This allows organizations to address potential issues early on.

Do you think John should have received coaching much earlier? How should organizations design executive coaching programmes for high-potential talent?

Yes, John should have received coaching earlier. Early intervention through coaching could have helped John maintain self-awareness and adaptability throughout his career, preventing the challenges he eventually faced. To help high-potential employees develop into well-rounded leaders, organizations should design executive coaching programmes with the following key elements:

- **Proactive coaching:** High-potential employees should receive coaching as soon as they are identified. Early coaching can help them develop the necessary skills and mindsets to navigate future challenges effectively.
- **Tailored programmes:** Executive coaching should be customized to the individual's strengths and development areas. It should include regular check-ins, goal setting, and structured reflection practices.
- **Integration with performance reviews:** Coaching should be linked with performance reviews to ensure

employees receive continuous feedback and guidance on their growth areas. This alignment helps reinforce development goals.

- **Focus on soft skills:** In additional to technical and business acumen, coaching should emphasize critical soft skills such as emotional intelligence, adaptability, and communication, which are essential for leadership success.

This reflection underscores the importance of continuous learning, self-awareness, and adaptability in leadership. It also highlights the need for organizations to implement strong talent management strategies that support long-term growth and success for their leaders.

6

Case Story 5
Shaping Strategy and Driving Change

Transforming an Aged Plant

Samrat was promoted to the role of plant head at one of the oldest plants in western India within a large multinational company. He had been with the company for many years and had held various roles across manufacturing, strategy, and product development. Since joining the organization, he had been fascinated by the impact of technology on business and had always sought to learn more, do more, and drive innovation whenever technology was involved. His curiosity for technology and passion for learning had been key factors in his consistently being promoted ahead of his peers and remaining on the fast track for career growth.

Samrat was a man of high intelligence who approached challenges differently and consistently integrated technology into his projects—whether in college, as a trainee in his early career, or later as a production manager. In every role he took on, his focus was on creating impact rather than merely improving efficiency or undertaking Herculean tasks for accolades. His approach to assignments was always to drive meaningful, long-lasting change, transforming each role into one that delivered tangible impact. This mindset led to him being entrusted with increasingly difficult assignments.

The role of plant head at the oldest plant was both an achievement and a formidable challenge. It was a celebratory milestone because Samrat was the youngest plant head in the plant's history, and the organization's trust in him at such a young age was certainly commendable. However, the role also came with significant difficulties. The plant was very old, much of the equipment was outdated, and technology had long been a weak area. Additionally, the union was volatile, and there had already been considerable hostility between management and the union. As it was one of the oldest plants, many employees had worked together for over thirty years, creating a highly political environment. Young recruits often sought opportunities elsewhere—either in other plants or different parts of the business—due to the bureaucracy and entrenched political culture.

On his first day in the role, Samrat sat among his team, addressing them. Many were former seniors he had once reported to, while others were individuals he had never liked due to their bureaucratic approach. Every positive note in his inaugural speech was met with a dull, indifferent, and despondent reaction from his direct reports, who made no effort to hide their disinterest in the ideas of the 'new kid on the block'. As the day progressed, his energy was steadily drained, and the excitement of his promotion and new role was gradually replaced by a sobering reality check.

On his way back, he found himself in a pensive mood, uncertain whether accepting this role was a boon or a bane. He kept reflecting on his strategy for the way forward—how to navigate the challenges at hand and transform the plant into a global lighthouse for the organization. Such was the scale of his ambitions and aspirations.

The next morning, on his way to the office, Samrat resolved not to dwell too much on the current situation. Instead, he decided to give himself ninety days to assess and address the challenges at hand. With this in mind, he began preparing his ninety-day plan.

He broadly understood the plant's challenges. The first was technology, the second was digitization and automation, and the third was the replacement of outdated machines and securing capital investment (Capex) to enable a safer, more technologically advanced product.

He realized that his team had been doing the same jobs for a long time and needed rotation. Some team members were highly knowledgeable, while others were younger and had aspirations. There were also those whom he felt did not add value to the team. However, he was determined to withhold judgement and set aside any biases from his previous role—whether about his team or any other business aspect. His approach was clear—he wanted to fully understand every aspect from a leadership perspective before deciding how to address the challenges.

As the ninety-day mark passed, Samrat realized he had been right about his team. He needed to retain the knowledgeable old-timers, ease out some low performers, and build a new team with fresh credo—'Dream Big, Deliver Bigger'.

On the union front, he observed that while the union was willing to work with the leadership, there was a significant trust deficit. To drive organizational outcomes together, he needed to foster trust and mutual respect. Clearly, the way forward was to collaborate with union leaders on a shared plan and establish faith in one another.

On the technology front, a complete revamp was necessary. Digital transformation and automation efforts had to be prioritized, and careful planning was required to secure Capex approval from corporate headquarters.

On the cultural front, fostering a learning-driven environment was essential. The focus needed to be on energizing the workplace, cultivating a growth mindset, and empowering younger employees. Another critical business imperative was improving productivity and safety, as the plant had consistently been flagged for high costs and safety violations.

As Samrat began writing his ninety-day report, his mind was filled with actionable steps. How should he address these challenges? If he reached out to his manager—a highly experienced leader in the organization—he would undoubtedly gain valuable insights. However, Samrat believed he already understood the core issues. He knew the plant well, having spent years there. He knew the people. The problem lay within the unit, and so did the solution. He needed to reflect on the path forward—initiating change, shaping strategy, and driving transformation.

The broad strategic priorities were outlined in five key areas: technology, culture, union management, safety, and productivity. Before unveiling the strategic framework and action plan, Samrat reached out to an old friend who worked at one of the most high-tech plants of a competitor. He arranged a visit for his team members and some promising young employees to gain exposure to advanced manufacturing practices.

The three-day visit allowed the team to reflect deeply and opened their minds to a world of possibilities. After returning, they presented their learnings to the larger extended team, highlighting key takeaways and potential improvements for their own plant. This shift in direction energized many younger team members, sparking their enthusiasm to learn more, contribute actively, and become part of the plant's reinvention journey.

Samrat noticed the positive momentum and decided to build on it by organizing a two-day workshop with the extended team to refine the strategic priorities. To encourage participation and idea generation, he ensured that the teams were formed in a diverse manner.

The workshop proved to be an ideal platform for both brainstorming and strengthening team dynamics. Over two days of discussions, the team collaboratively shaped and finalized the strategic priorities.

As Samrat advanced the strategic plan, he handpicked a group of twenty young emerging leaders and integrated them into key focus areas alongside his direct reports. Each was empowered to drive outcomes and was included in leadership team meetings whenever discussions were relevant to their area of work.

Over time, these young leaders, with their energy, commitment, and sharp focus on goals, began driving meaningful change. Their momentum spurred the seasoned veterans into action, gradually shifting the organization dynamic. Step by step, milestone after milestone, the team worked together to shape the transformation.

Along the way, several tough decisions had to be made—easing out underperformers, enforcing discipline through consequence management, engaging with the union on outsourcing models to enhance productivity, shifting certain operations to vendor bases instead of in-house production, and rationalizing vendors based on quality and cost considerations.

Over three years of intense, high-impact work, the plant had transformed into a lighthouse of excellence across all its strategic focus areas. Samrat thrived in the energy of the workplace, fuelled by a flurry of recognitions.

One day, he received a call inviting him to move to headquarters to lead operations for the entire company. As the call ended, he smiled to himself. While he was gratified that his hard work had earned him the reward he had aimed for, his smile also reflected the anticipation of the next challenge. His journey had been like that of a general—moving from one battleground to another, always protecting and advancing the company's interests.

Points for Reflection

- What did Samrat do right, and why?
- Which of his actions demonstrate shaping strategy and managing change?
- Is there anything more that Samrat could have done?
- Why was it important for Samrat to engage young emerging leaders?

Author's Perspective on the Case Story

What did Samrat do right, and why?

- **Focus on learning and technology:** Samrat's lifelong fascination with technology enabled him to recognize its potential to transform the plant. By prioritizing technological upgrades, he laid the foundation for innovation.
- **Comprehensive ninety-day plan:** Instead of rushing into decisions, he took the time to assess the situation, allowing him to understand the complexities of the plant and team dynamics before implementing changes.
- **Engagement with the team:** His decision to involve his team in a visit to a high-tech plant broadened their perspective and invigorated their enthusiasm, fostering a collaborative and forward-thinking work environment.
- **Empowerment of young leaders:** By handpicking and empowering emerging young leaders, he not only motivated the next generation but also infused fresh ideas and energy into the workplace, ensuring long-term transformation.
- **Strategic workshops:** Organizing a two-day workshop was a smart move that leveraged collective intelligence, encouraged ownership among team members, and strengthened accountability.

Which of his actions demonstrate shaping strategy and managing change?

- **Identifying key areas for improvement:** Samrat outlined strategic priorities in technology, culture, union management, safety, and productivity, demonstrating a clear and structured vision for transformation.
- **Building trust with unions:** Recognizing the trust deficit, he actively worked to improve relations with union leaders, showing a commitment to collaborative change and long-term stability.
- **Continuous evaluation and adaptation:** Regularly assessing team dynamics and performance allowed him to make necessary adjustments, such as easing out non-performers and optimizing team structure.
- **Milestone-driven approach:** Setting and achieving specific milestones helped maintain momentum, ensuring sustained progress and motivating the team to strive for continuous improvement.

Is there something more that Samrat could have done?

- **Enhanced communication:** While he engaged with his team, ongoing transparent communication about challenges and progress could have further solidified trust and alignment across all levels.
- **Fostering a more inclusive culture:** Beyond involving young leaders, creating platforms for all employees to voice their ideas and concerns might have enriched the change process and strengthened team cohesion.
- **Developing a formal mentorship programme:** Implementing a structured mentorship programme could have accelerated the development of both young

talent and seasoned employees, ensuring knowledge transfer and long-term leadership continuity.

Why was it important for Samrat to engage young emerging leaders?

- **Fresh perspectives:** Young leaders bring innovative ideas and new approaches that challenge the status quo, which is crucial for driving transformation.
- **Motivating the workforce:** Their involvement can inspire other employees, creating a ripple effect that enhances overall morale and productivity.
- **Succession planning:** Engaging young talent prepares them for future leadership roles, ensuring continuity and stability within the organization.
- **Cultural shift:** Empowering young leaders helps shift the organizational culture towards one that values agility, learning, and collaboration—essential for a modern workplace.

In summary, Samrat's strategic approach and commitment to empowering his team were instrumental in transforming the plant. While he succeeded in many areas, maintaining continuous communication and fostering greater inclusion could have further strengthened his leadership journey. Engaging young leaders was crucial not only for immediate impact but also for cultivating a sustainable, innovative culture for the future.

About the Author

Biswaroop Mukherjee is an experienced HR leader. He has handled multiple high-impact roles in the domain of HR in various organizations of repute across industries and geographies. Biswaroop's journey in HR began with a passion for understanding the intricacies of human behaviour in the workplace and a drive to create positive organizational cultures that foster growth and development. His interests and expertise are wide ranging, encompassing such eclectic fields as organization development, change management, executive coaching, and building high-performing teams. His book *Apostles: A Candid Take on Managing Organisations and Talent*, also published by BluOne Ink, is a bestseller in its category.

Biswaroop completed his management education from SIBM, Pune, and bachelor's in science from Fergusson College, Pune. He is Vice President (People and Transformation) at global energy firm Aker Solutions. Before this, he was the HR head at Tata Motors, where he worked for over a decade. He has also worked at GE, Deloitte, Dr. Reddy's, and ABP Group.

An ICF-certified coach and a Hogan-certified assessor, he has developed a keen interest in human resource development and management. His diverse background equips him with a unique perspective on the challenges and opportunities facing HR practitioners in today's fast-paced and ever-changing business environment. Driven by a commitment to continuous learning and professional development, Biswaroop earned certifications in executive coaching and assessment and regularly participates in industry conferences and workshops.

9 789365 473766

Printed at Repro India Ltd.